PLAYBACK+
Speed • Pitch • Balance • Loop

ADELE

T0066161

To access audio visit:
www.halleonard.com/mylibrary

"Enter Code"
8207-0542-8710-6927

Cover photo by: Dana Edelson/NBC/NBCU Photo Bank via Getty Images

ISBN 978-1-4950-5813-4

HAL•LEONARD®
CORPORATION
7777 W. BLUEMOUND RD. P.O. BOX 13819 MILWAUKEE, WI 53213

Visit Hal Leonard Online at
www.halleonard.com

CONTENTS

CHASING PAVEMENTS

Words and Music by ADELE ADKINS
and FRANCIS EG WHITE

Moderately slow

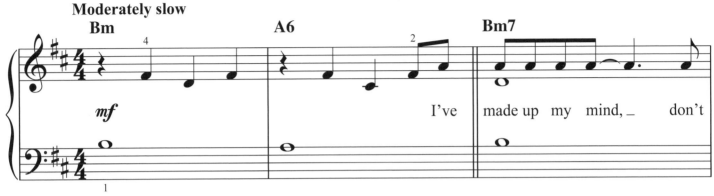

mf

With pedal

I've made up my mind,_ don't

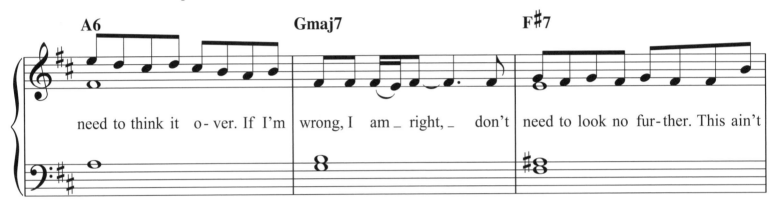

need to think it o-ver. If I'm wrong, I am _ right, _ don't need to look no fur-ther. This ain't

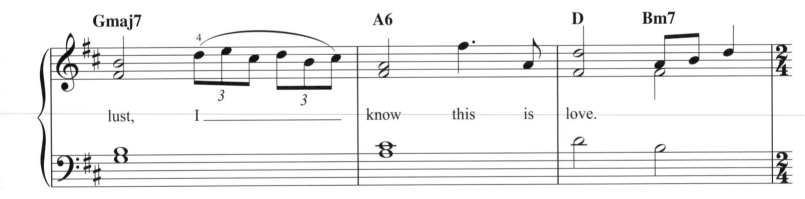

lust, I _____ know this is love.

But if I tell the world, _ I'll nev-er say e-nough, 'cause it was
build my-self up _____ and fly a-round in cir-cles, wait-ing

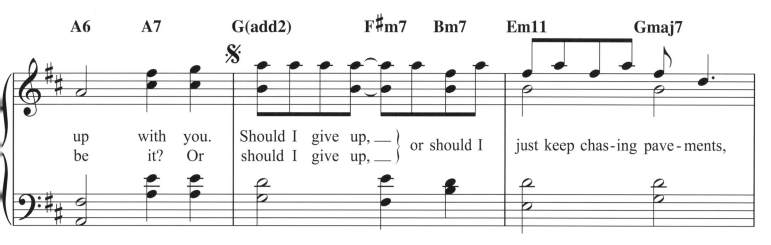

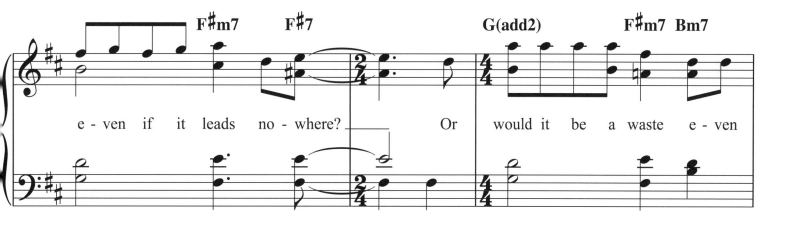

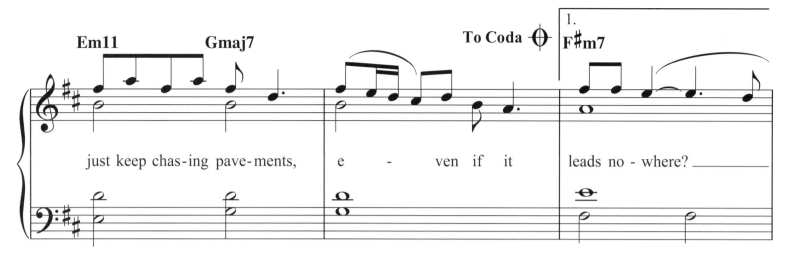

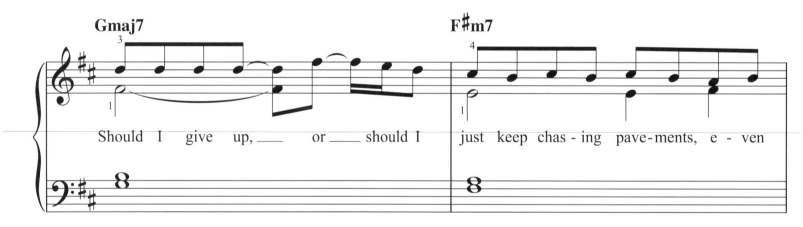

knew my place? _ Should I leave it there? _____ Should I _____

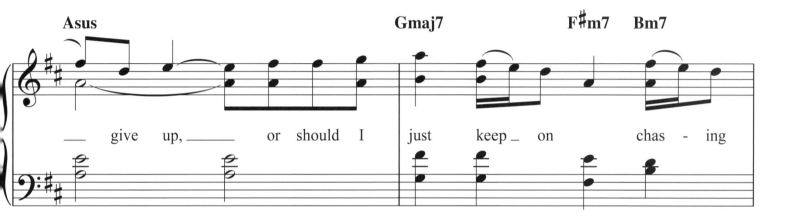

___ give up, _____ or should I just keep _ on chas - ing

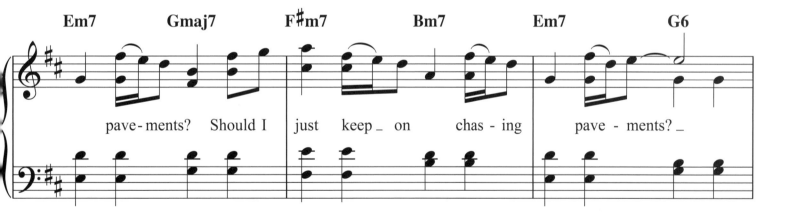

pave - ments? Should I just keep _ on chas - ing pave - ments? _

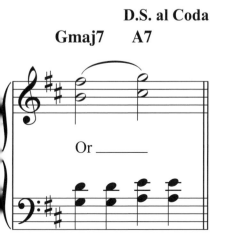

D.S. al Coda

Or _____

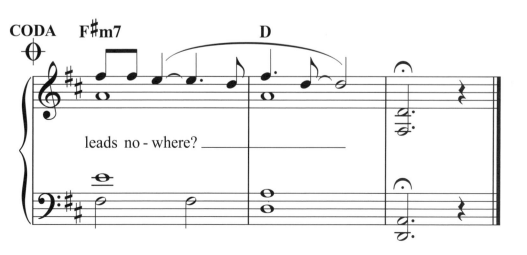

leads no - where? _____

HELLO

Words and Music by ADELE ADKINS
and GREG KURSTIN

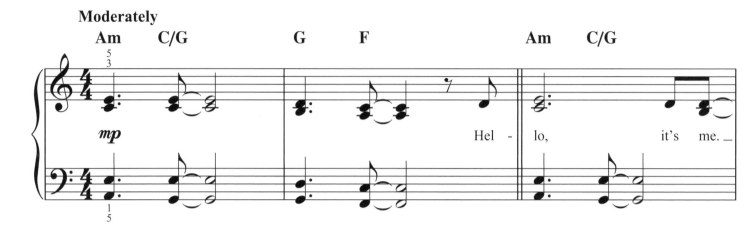

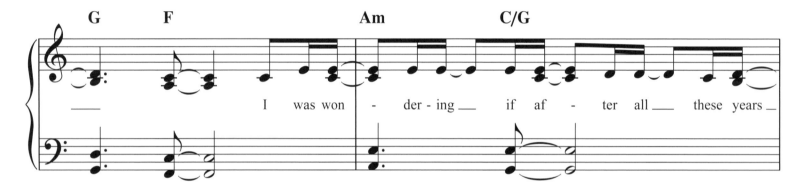

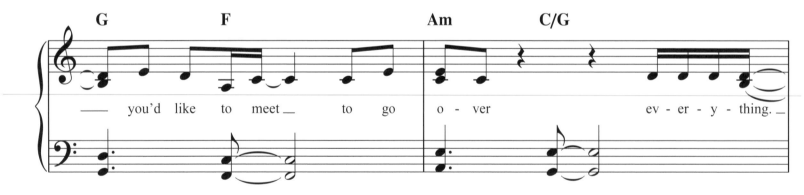

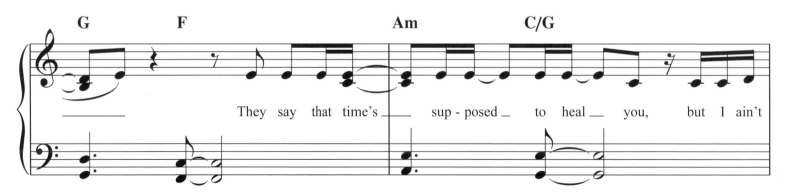

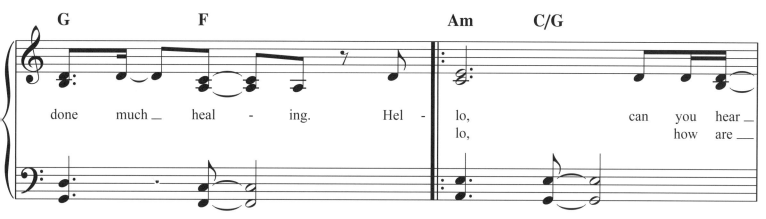

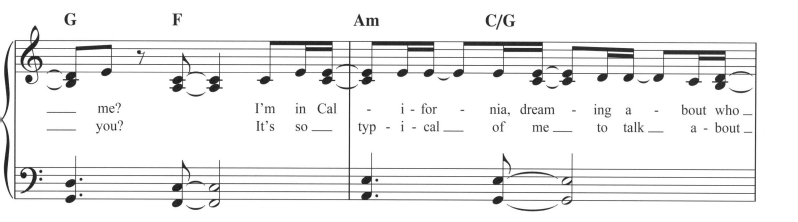

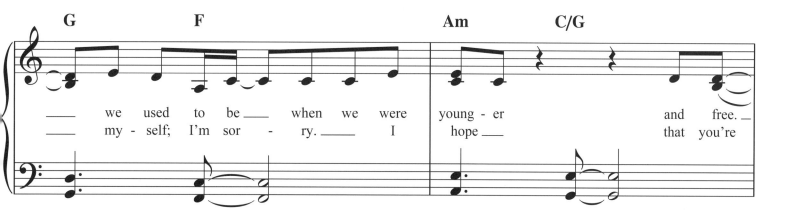

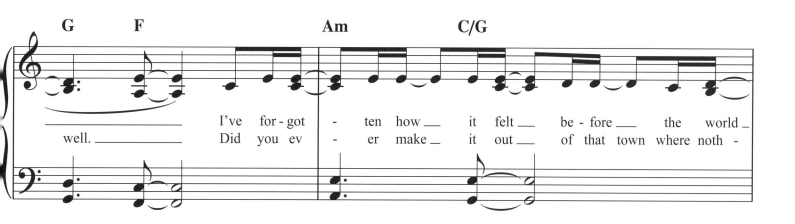

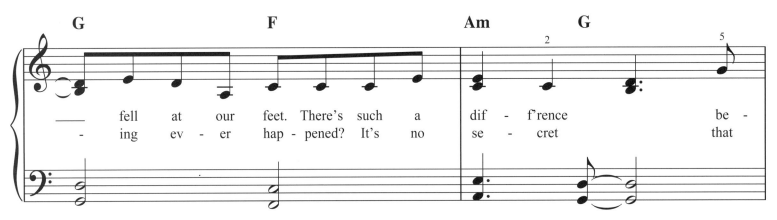

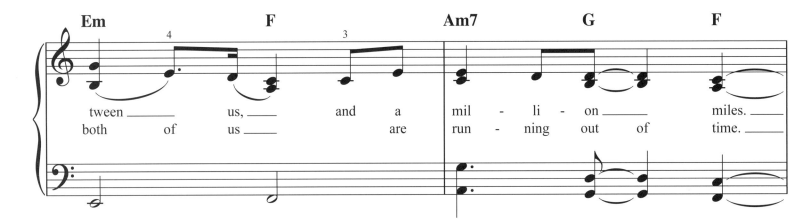

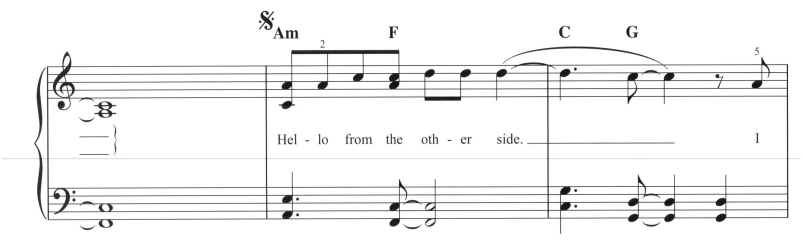

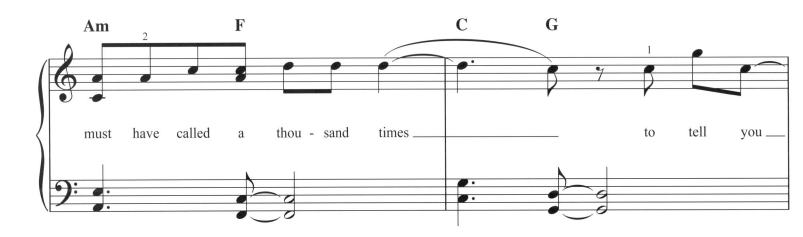

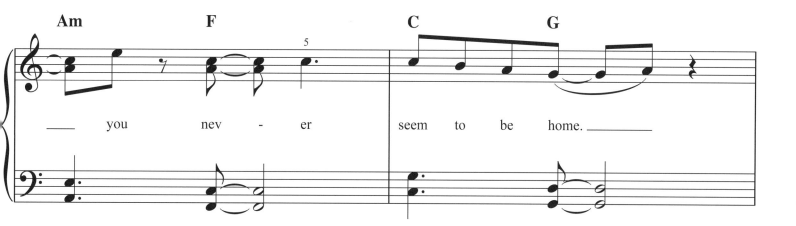

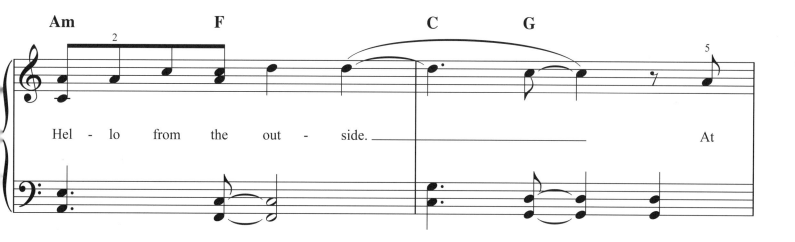

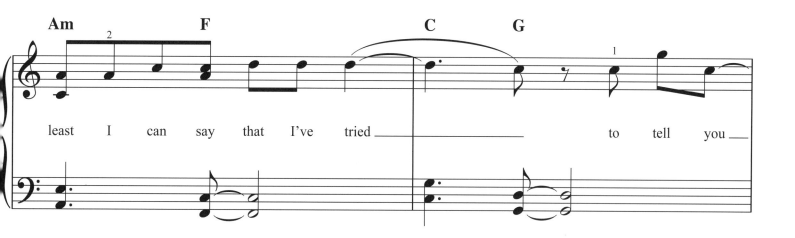

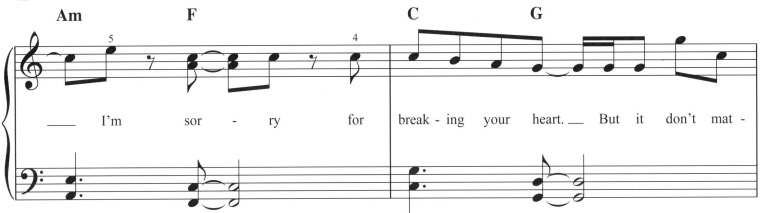

I'm sor - ry for breaking your heart.___ But it don't mat -

To Coda ⊕

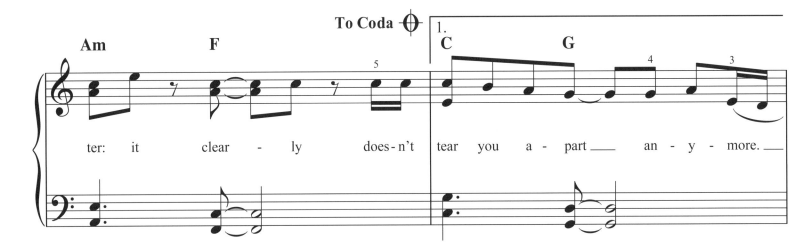

ter: it clear - ly does-n't tear you a - part___ an - y - more.___

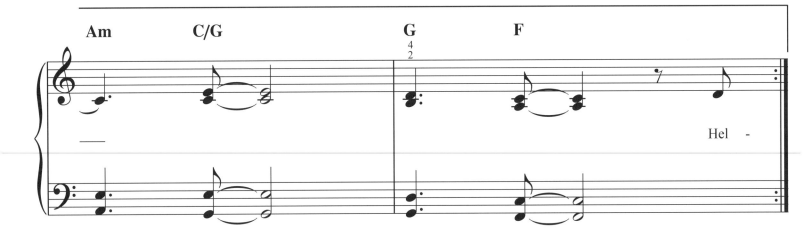

___ Hel -

tear you a - part___ an - y - more.___

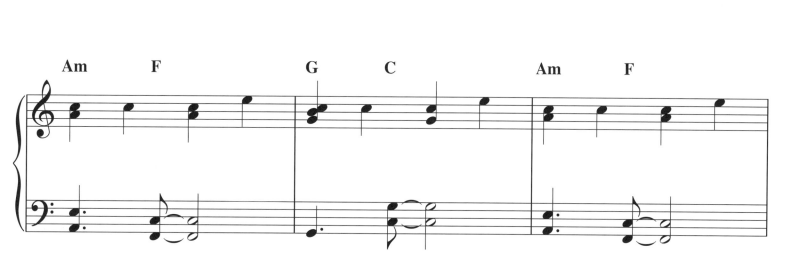

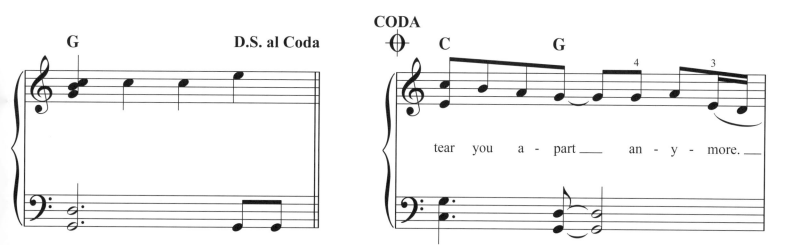

tear you a - part___ an - y - more.___

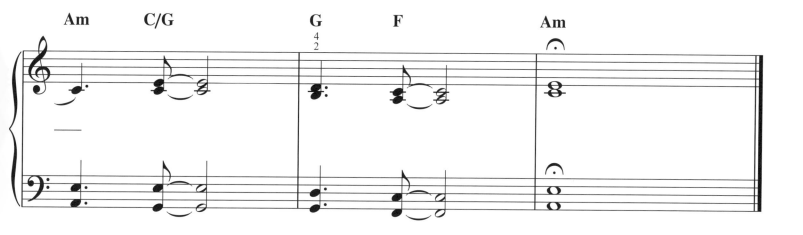

MAKE YOU FEEL MY LOVE

Words and Music by
BOB DYLAN

Moderately slow

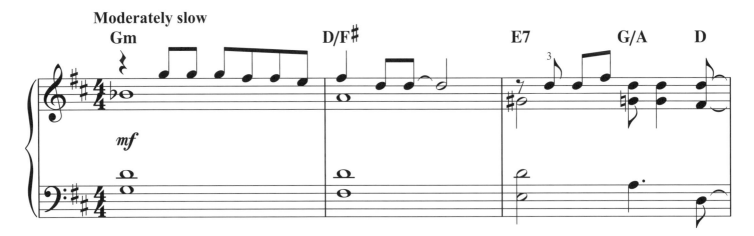

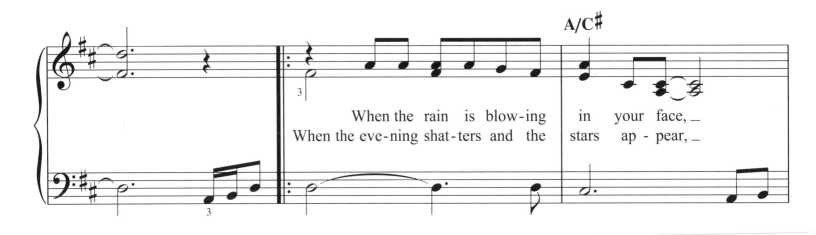

When the rain is blow-ing in your face, __
When the eve-ning shat-ters and the stars ap - pear, __

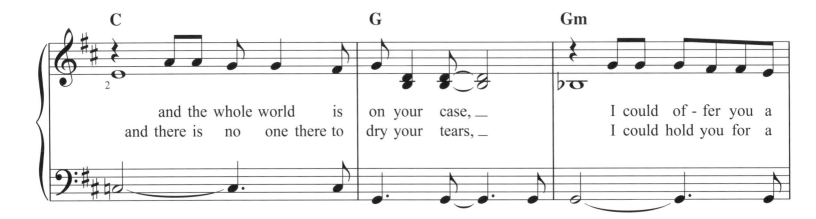

and the whole world is on your case, __
and there is no one there to dry your tears, __

I could of - fer you a
I could hold you for a

warm em - brace _
mil - lion years _
to make you feel my love. _
to make you feel my love. _

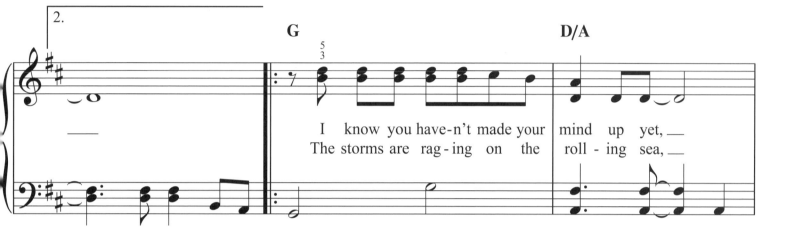

I know you have-n't made your mind up yet, _
The storms are rag-ing on the roll - ing sea, _

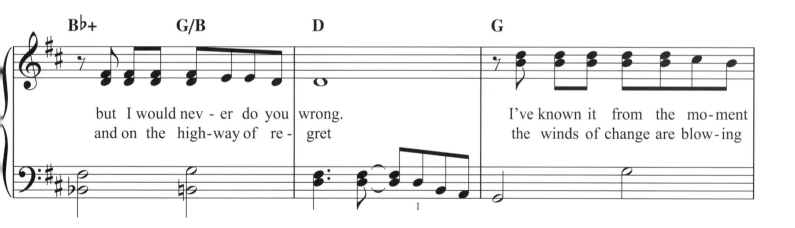

but I would nev - er do you wrong.
and on the high-way of re - gret
I've known it from the mo-ment
the winds of change are blow-ing

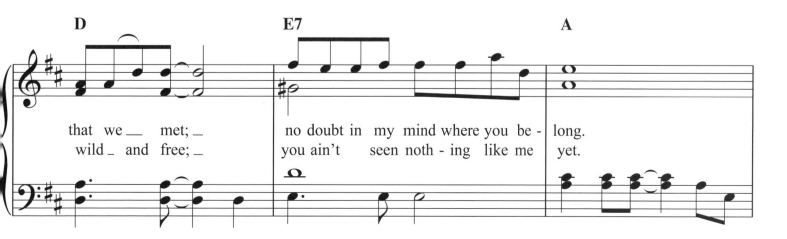

that we _ met; _
wild _ and free; _
no doubt in my mind where you be - long.
you ain't seen noth - ing like me yet.

I'd go hun-gry, I'd go black and blue, __ I'd go crawl-ing down the
I could make you hap-py, make your dreams come true, __ noth-ing that __ I __

av - e - nue. __ Know there's noth-ing that I would - n't do __
would-n't do. __ Go to the ends of the earth for you __

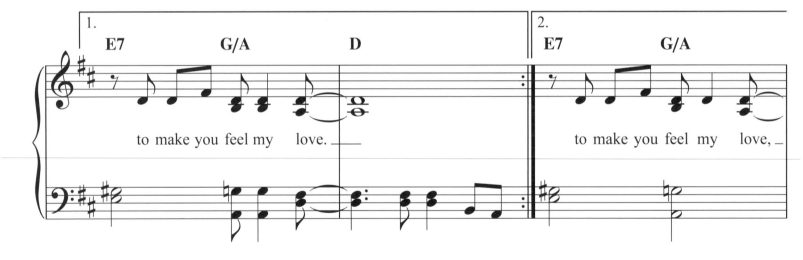

to make you feel my love. __ to make you feel my love, __

rit.

to make you feel my love. __

RUMOUR HAS IT

Words and Music by ADELE ADKINS
and RYAN TEDDER

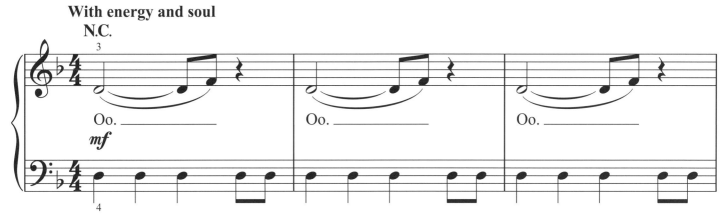

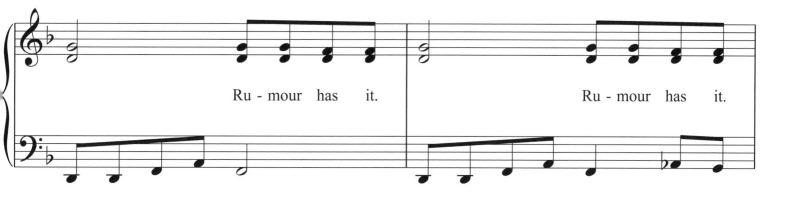

Ru - mour has it. Ru - mour has it.

To Coda ⊕

Ru - mour has it. Ru - mour. _____

She _____ is half your

age, but I'm gues - sing that's the rea - son that you _____

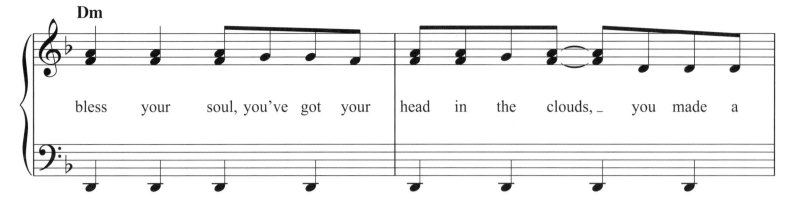

Dm

bless your soul, you've got your head in the clouds, _ you made a

Gm7

fool out of me ___ and boy, you're bring-ing me down. _ You made my

B♭maj7

Dm/A

heart melt, yet I'm cold to the core, ___ but

Gm7

D.S. al Coda

ru-mour has it I'm the one you're leav-ing her for. Ru-mour has it.

CODA

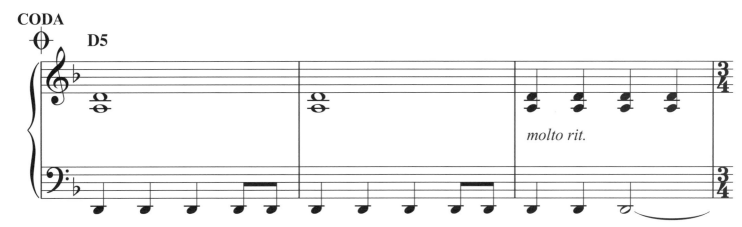

molto rit.

Much slower

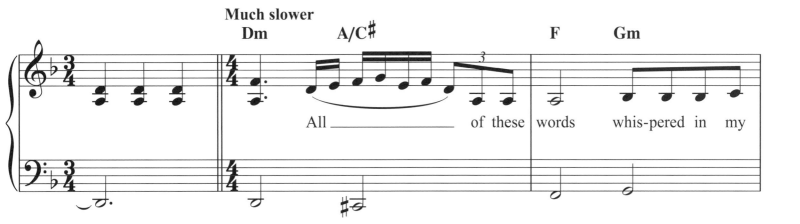

All _____ of these words whis-pered in my

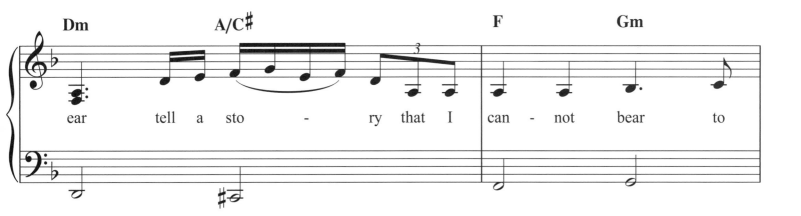

ear tell a sto - ry that I can - not bear to

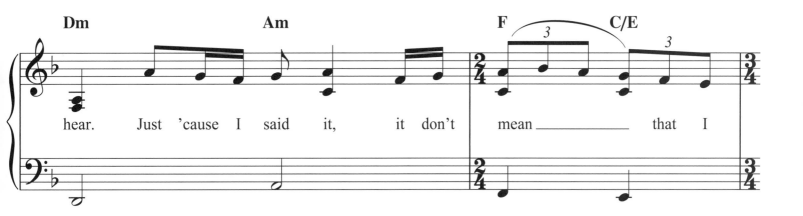

hear. Just 'cause I said it, it don't mean _____ that I

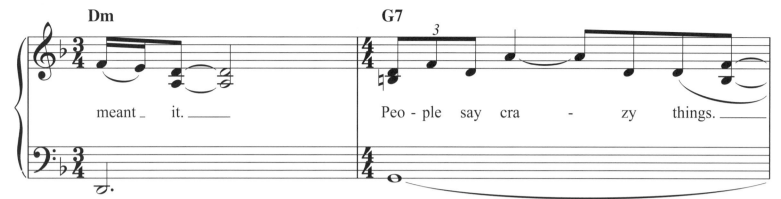

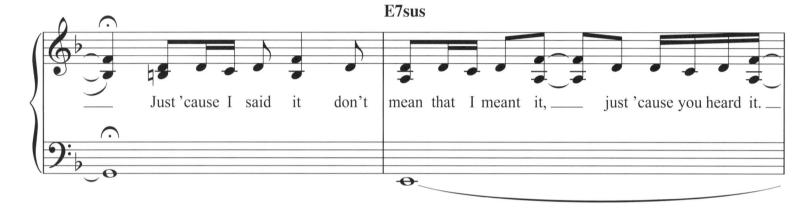

Ru - mour has it.

Ru - mour has it.

1.

Ru - mour has it.

Ru - mour has it.

Ru-mour has it. Ru - mour. __

2.

Ru-mour has it.

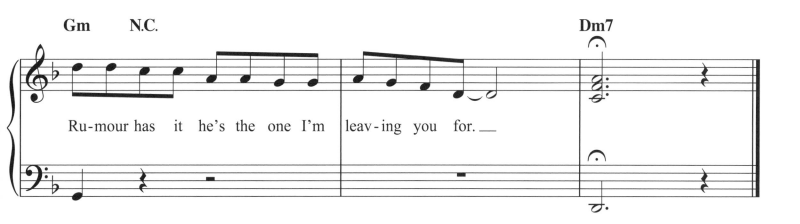

Gm   **N.C.**   **Dm7**

Ru-mour has it he's the one I'm leav-ing you for. __

REMEDY

Words and Music by ADELE ADKINS
and RYAN TEDDER

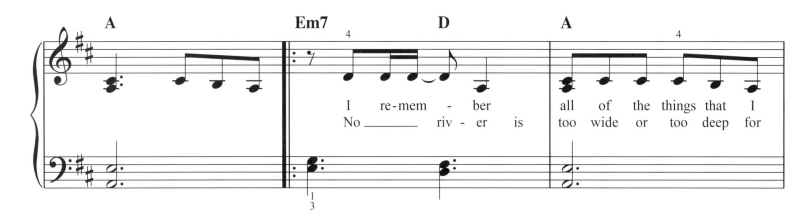

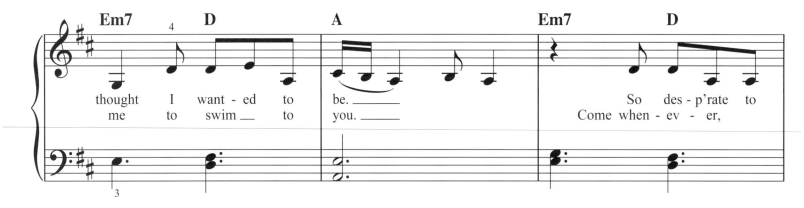

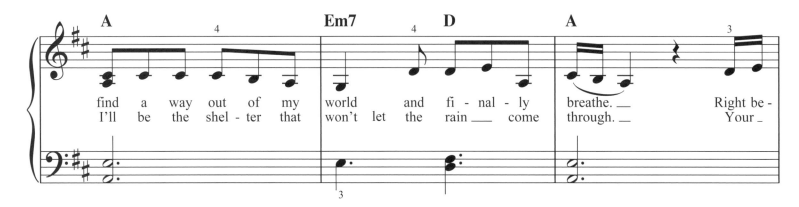

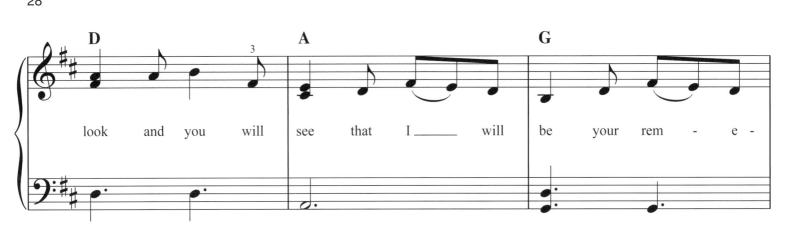

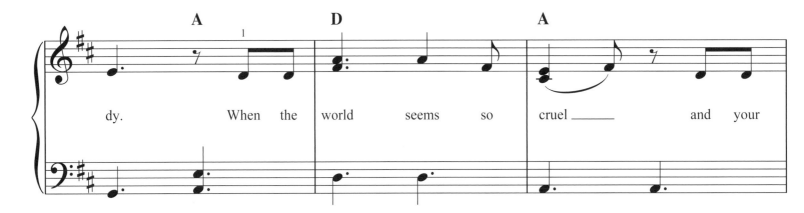

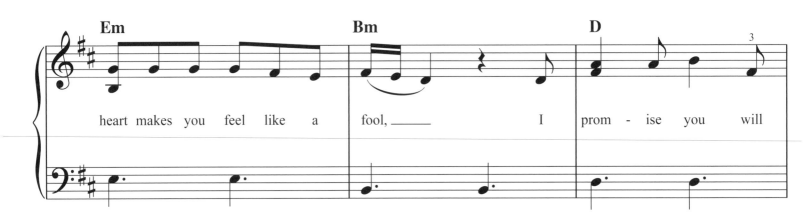

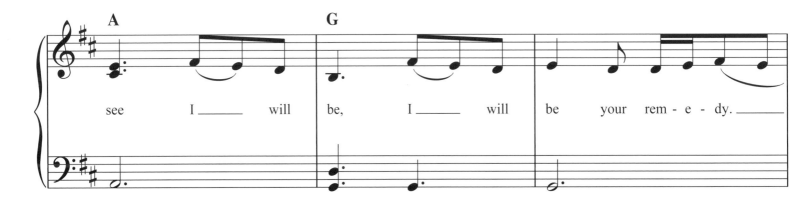

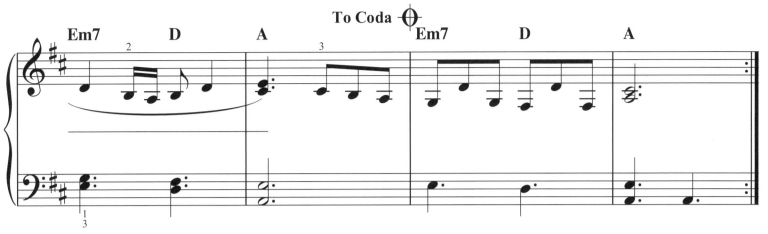

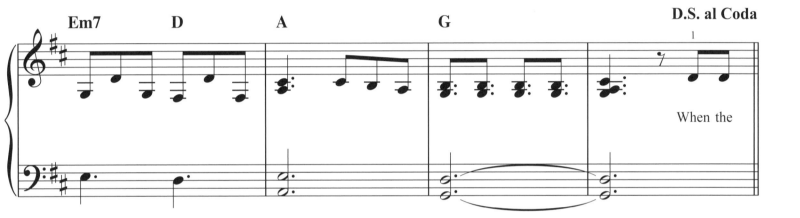

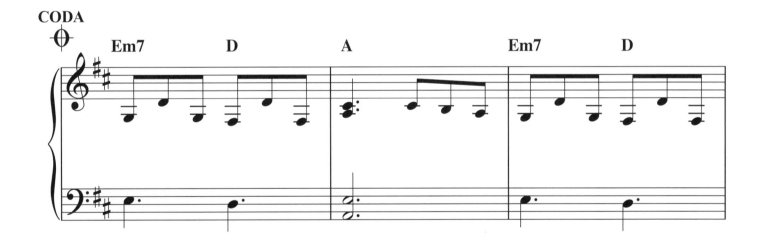

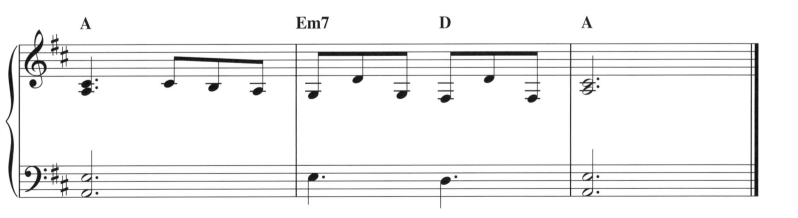

ROLLING IN THE DEEP

Words and Music by ADELE ADKINS
and PAUL EPWORTH

Soul groove

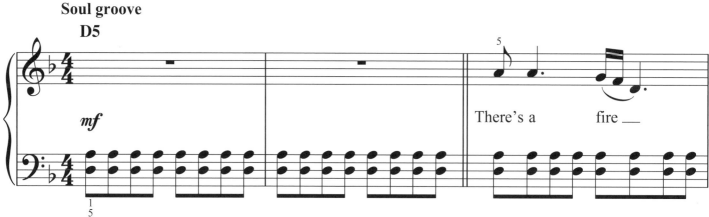

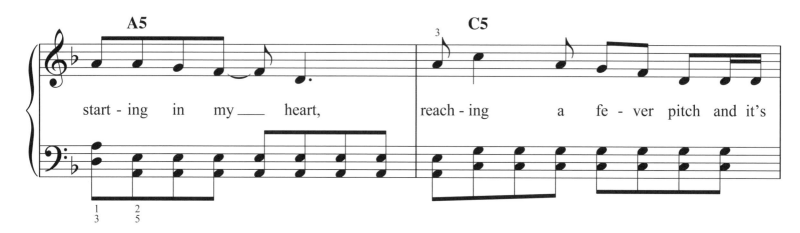

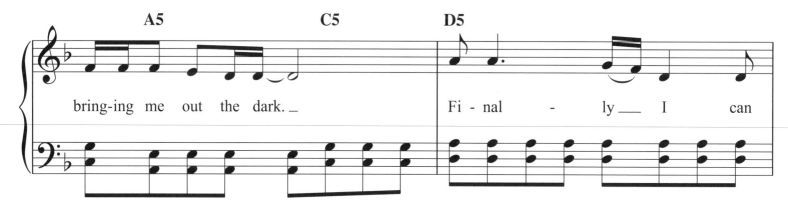

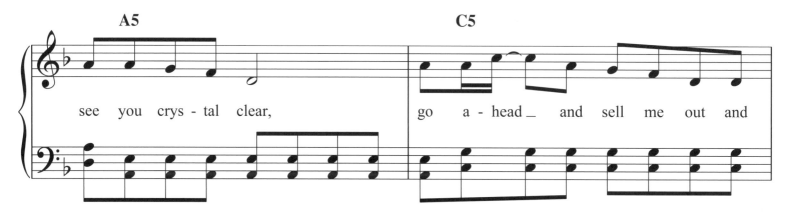

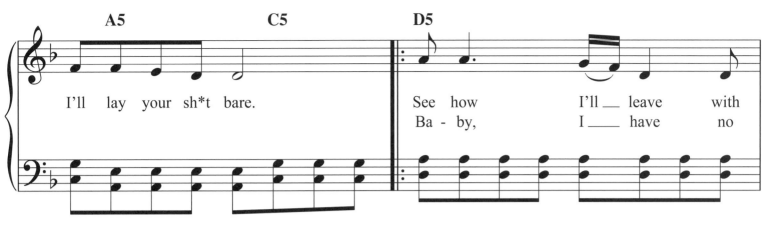

A5 C5 D5

I'll lay your sh*t bare.

See how I'll __ leave with
Ba - by, I ___ have no

A5 C5

ev - er - y piece of you,
sto - ry to be told, but

don't un - der - es - ti - mate the
I've heard one on you and I'm

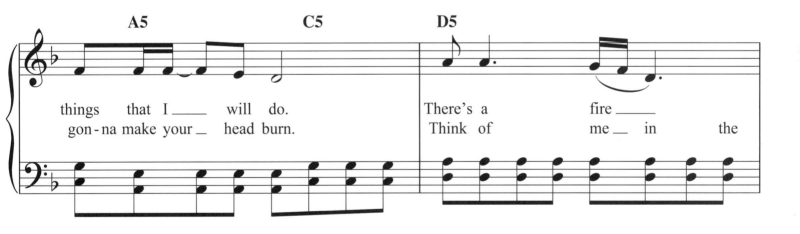

A5 C5 D5

things that I ___ will do.
gon - na make your __ head burn.

There's a fire ___
Think of me __ in the

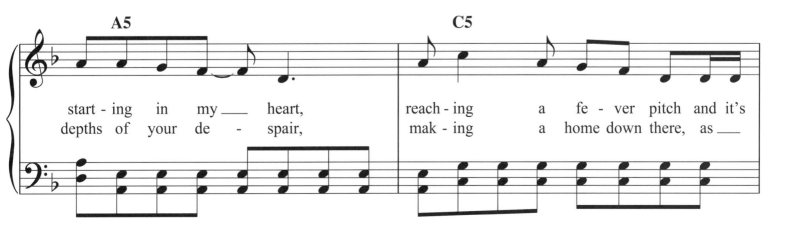

A5 C5

start - ing in my ___ heart,
depths of your de - spair,

reach - ing a fe - ver pitch and it's
mak - ing a home down there, as ___

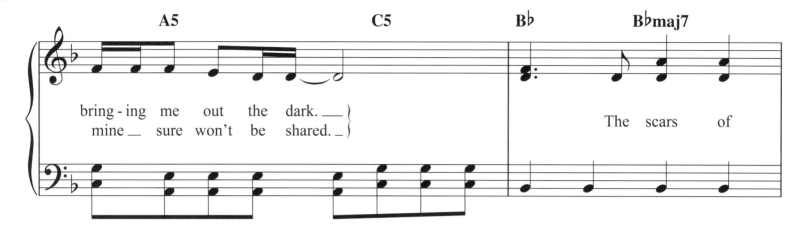

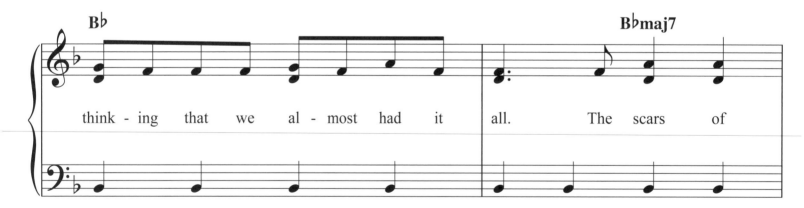

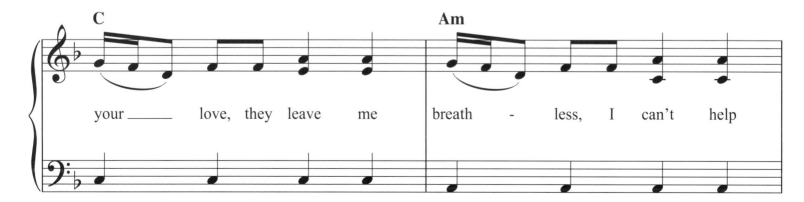

feel - ing   we could have had it   all, _____

_____   roll - ing   in   the   deep. _____

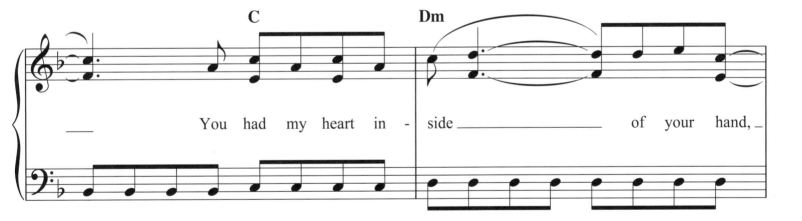

_____   You had my heart in - side _____ of your hand, _

_____   and you played _____ it _____ to the beat. _____

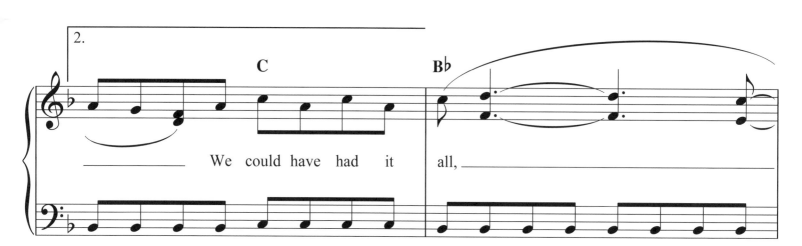

We could have had it all, _____

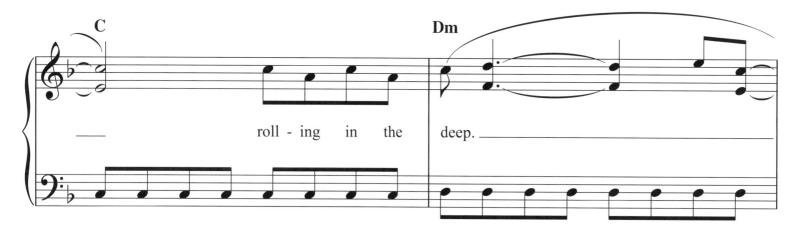

roll - ing in the deep. _____

You had my heart in - side _____ of your hand, __

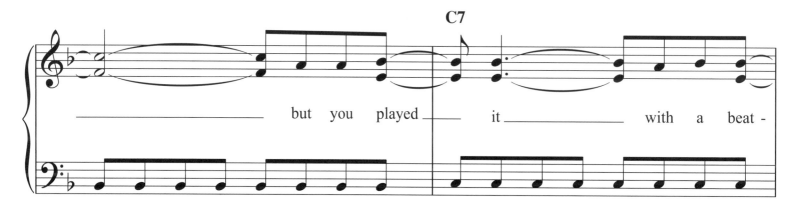

_____ but you played ___ it _____ with a beat -

C   **N.C.**

- ing...   Throw your   soul _____ through

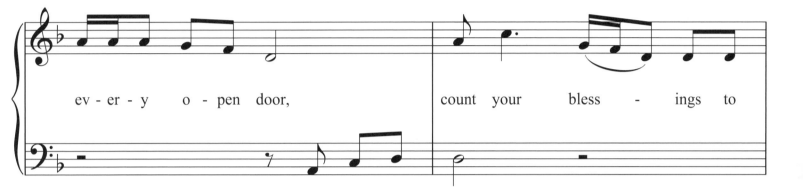

ev - er - y   o - pen door,   count your   bless — ings to

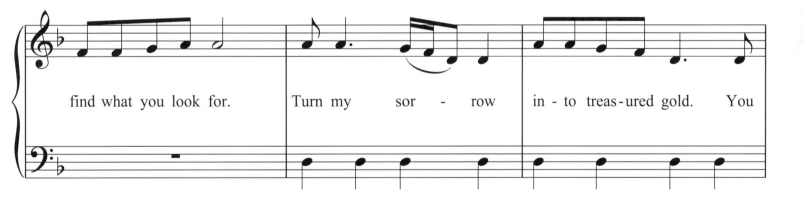

find what you look for.   Turn my   sor - row   in - to treas-ured gold.   You

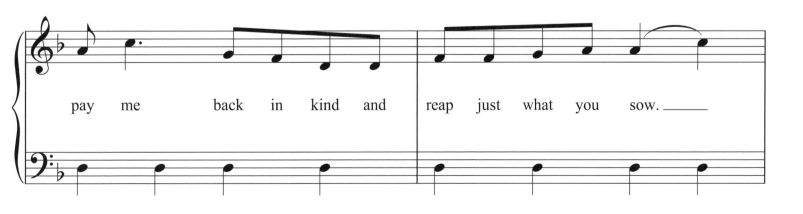

pay me   back in kind and   reap just what you sow. _____

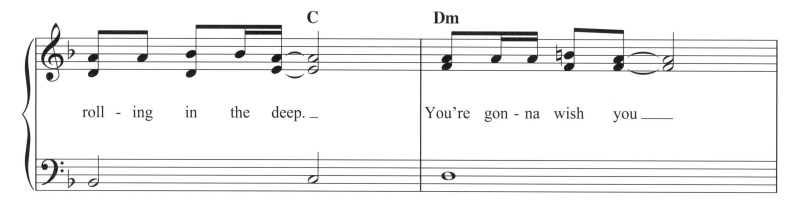

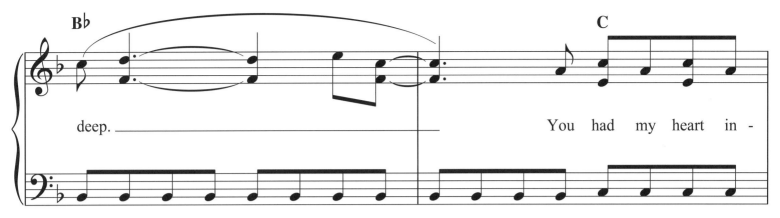

deep. _____ You had my heart in -

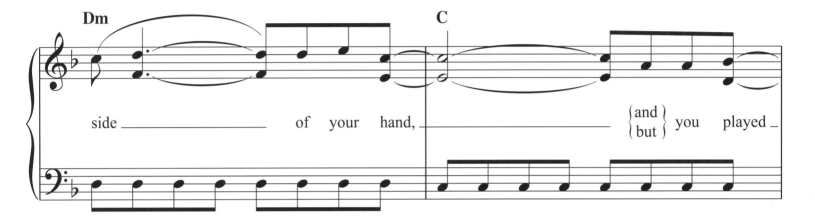

side _____ of your hand, _____ { and / but } you played _

1.

_ it _____ to the beat. _____ We could have had it

2.

_ it, you played _ it, you played _ it, you played _ it to the beat. _____

SET FIRE TO THE RAIN

Words and Music by ADELE ADKINS
and FRASER SMITH

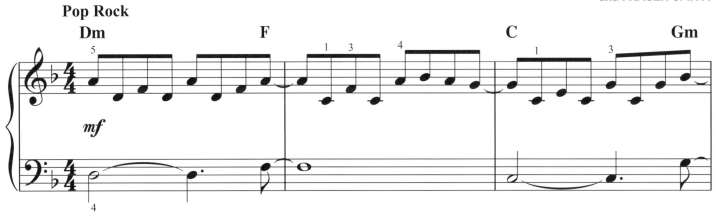

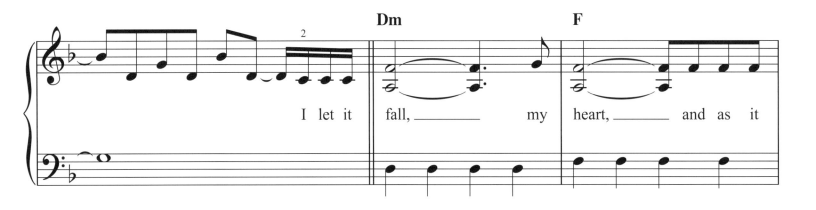

I let it fall, _____ my heart, _____ and as it

fell, you rose to claim ___ it. ___ It was dark _____ and I was o-

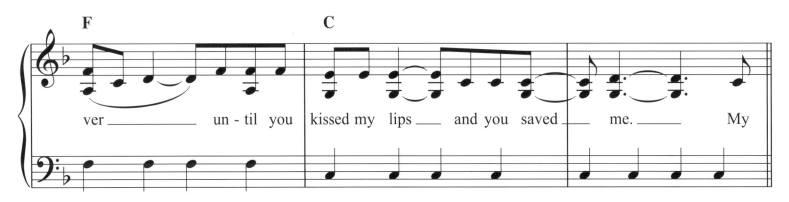

ver _____ un - til you kissed my lips ___ and you saved ___ me. _____ My

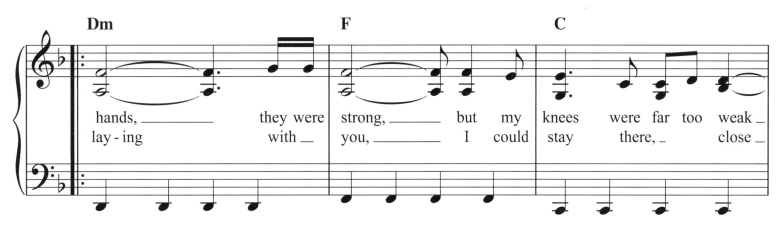

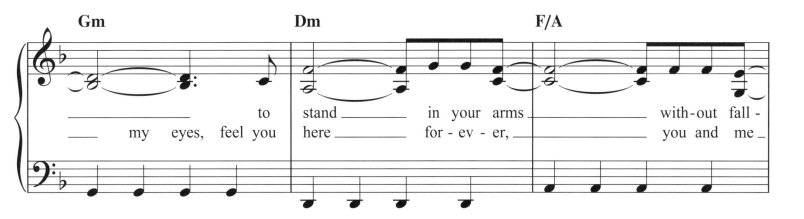

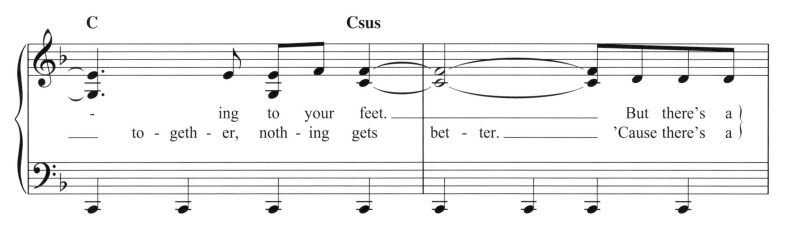

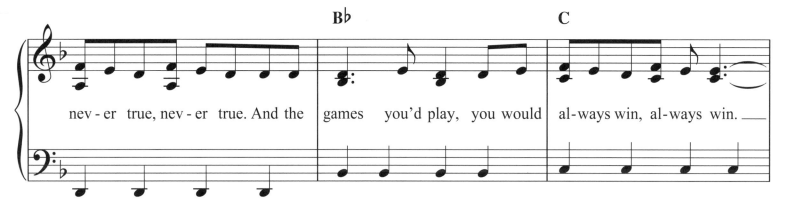

nev-er true, nev-er true. And the games you'd play, you would al-ways win, al-ways win. ___

___ But I set fire ___ to the rain, ___ watched it pour ___

___ as I ___ touched your face. ___ Well, it burned ___

___ while I cried, ___ 'cause I heard ___ it scream - ing out your

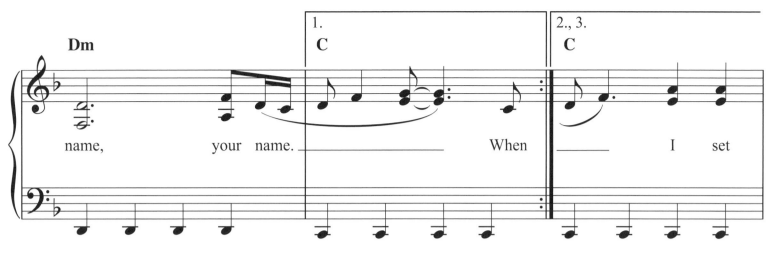

Dm name, your name. **1.** **C** When I set

2., 3. **C**

Dm fire to the rain and I threw us **C** in - to the flames.

Well, I felt some - thing die, 'cause I knew **Gm7**

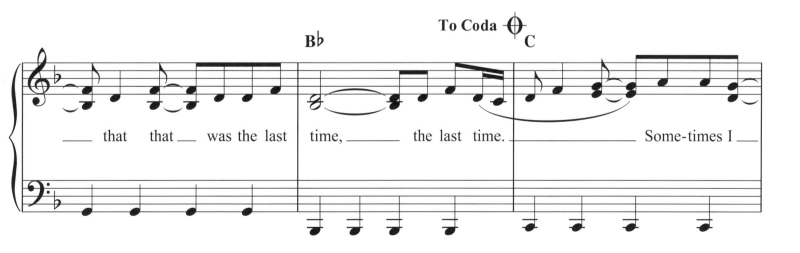

that that was the last **Bb** time, the last time. **To Coda** **C** Some-times I

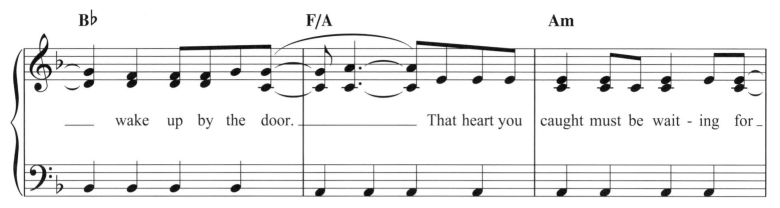

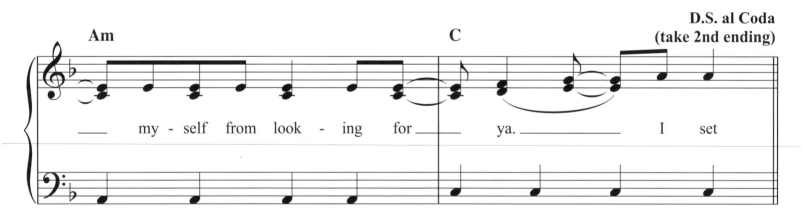

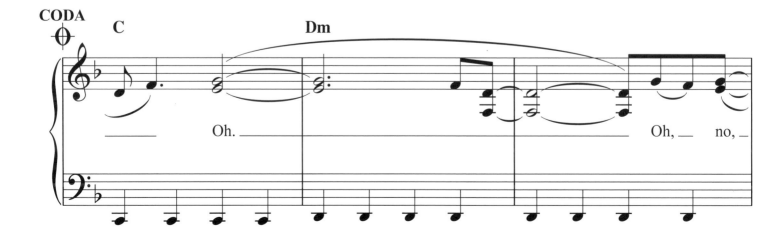

oh. _____ Let it burn. _____

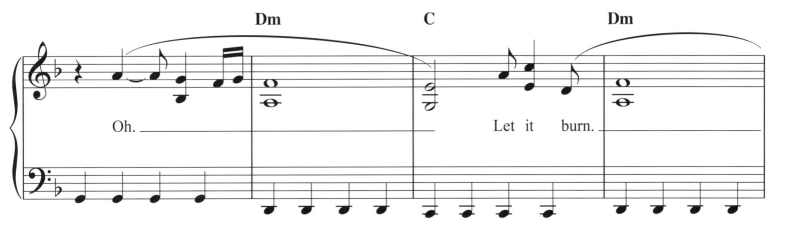

Oh. _____ Let it burn.

Let it burn. _____

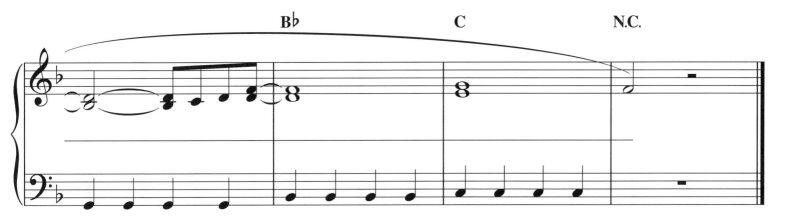

SKYFALL
from the Motion Picture SKYFALL

Words and Music by ADELE ADKINS
and PAUL EPWORTH

Slow, mysterious

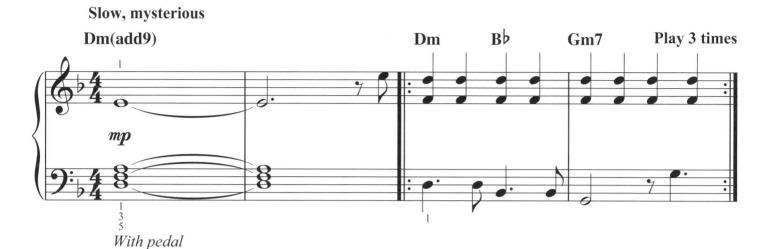

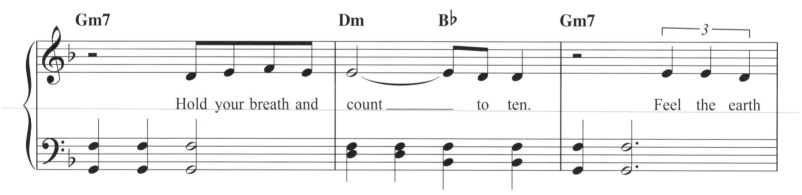

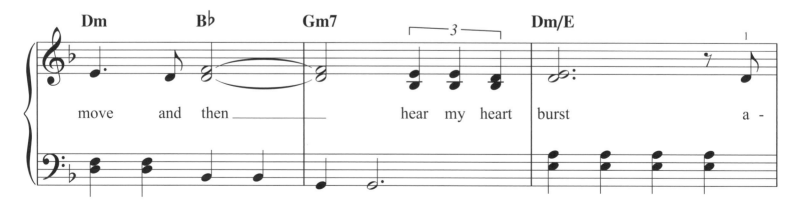

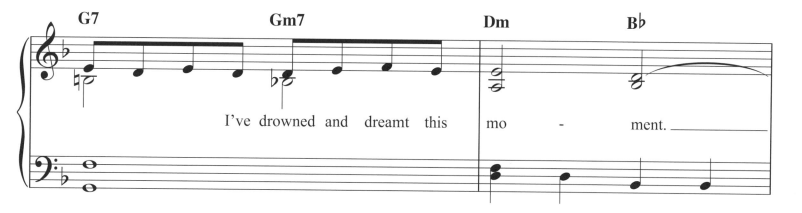

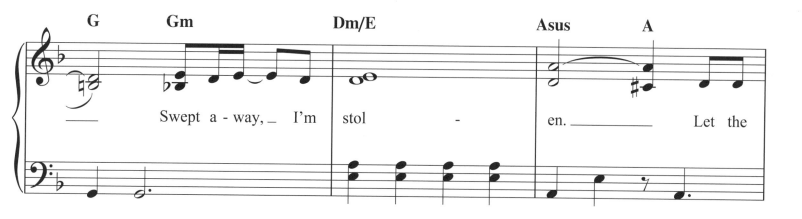

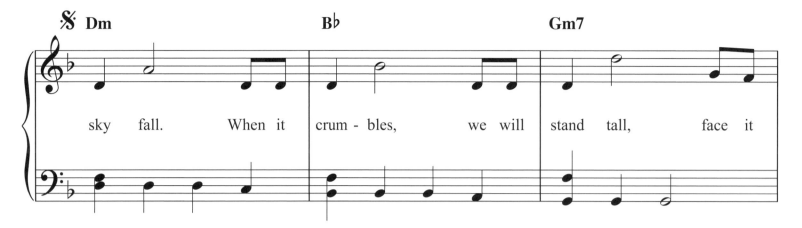

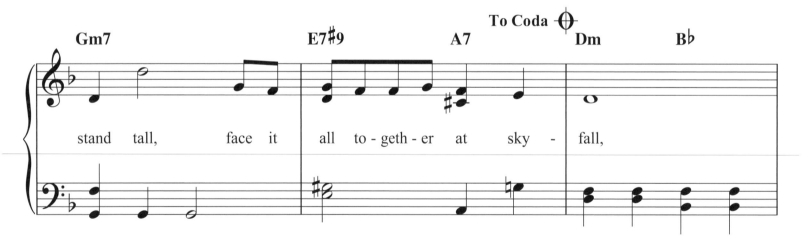

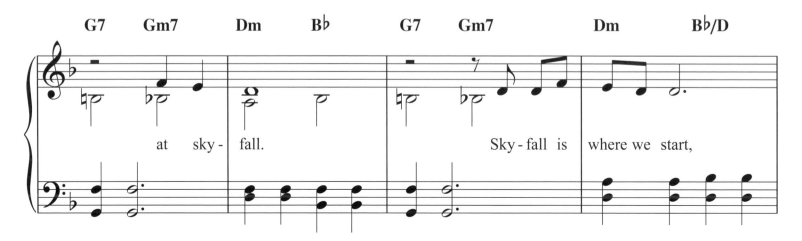

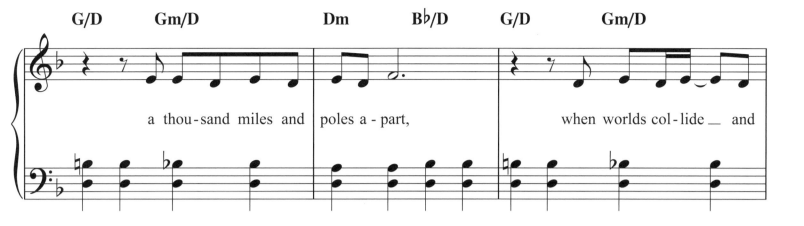

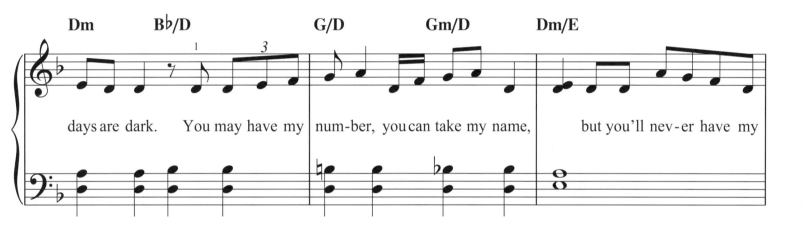

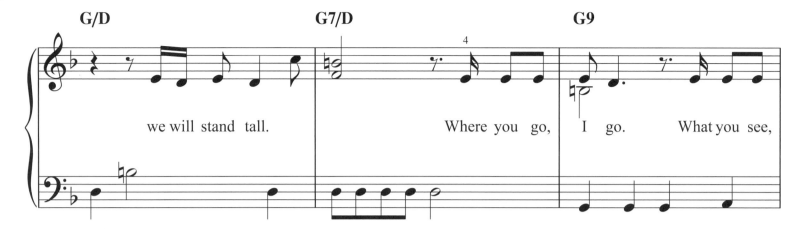

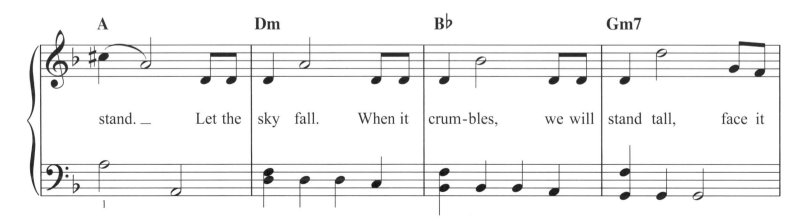

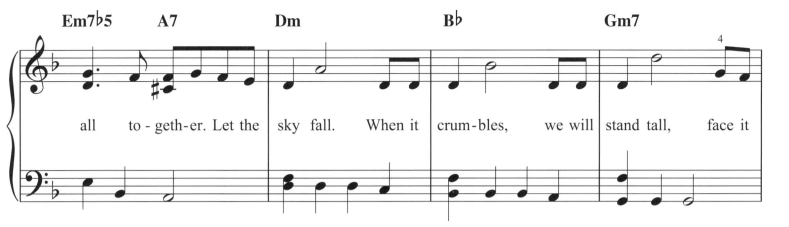

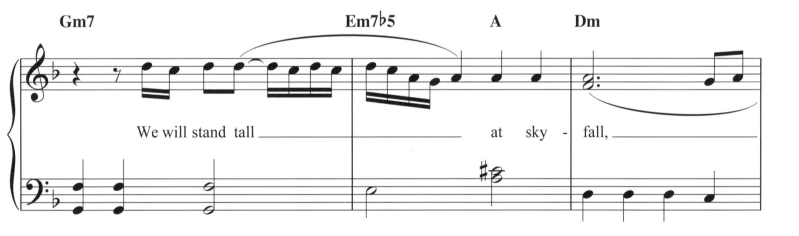

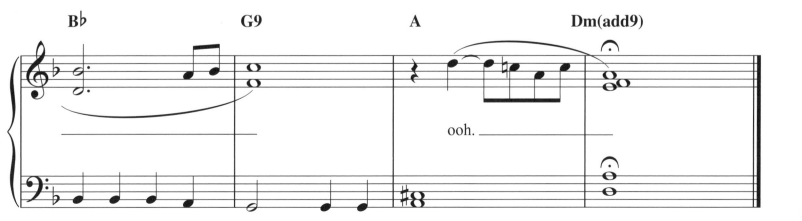

SOMEONE LIKE YOU

Words and Music by ADELE ADKINS
and DAN WILSON

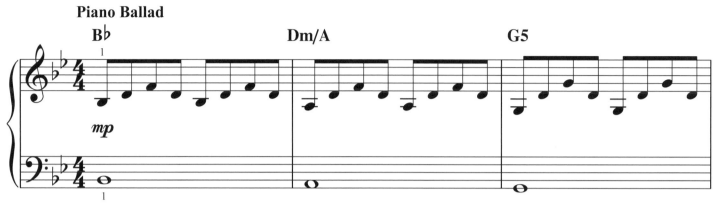

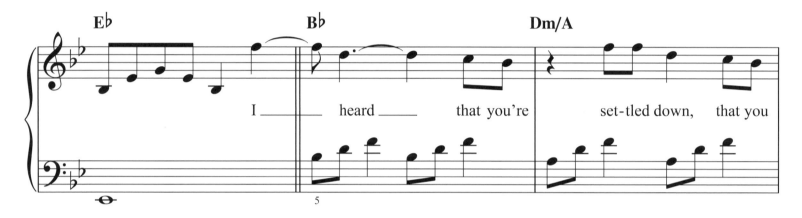

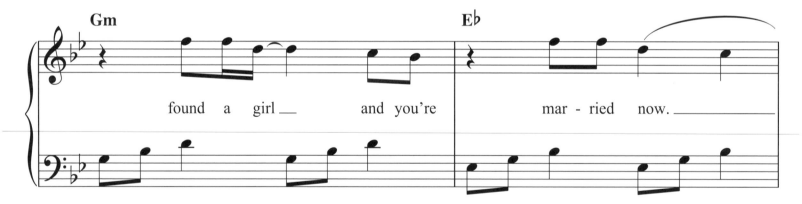

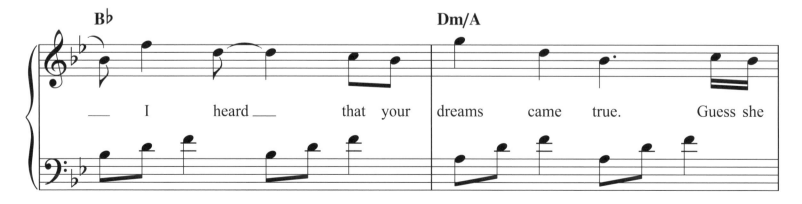

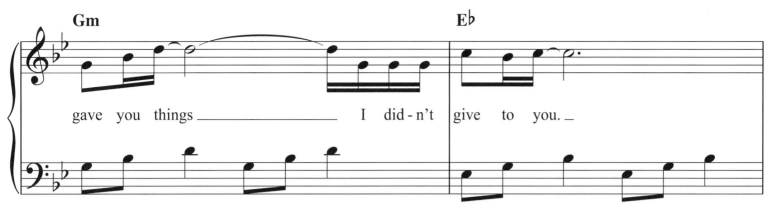

gave you things _____ I did-n't give to you. _

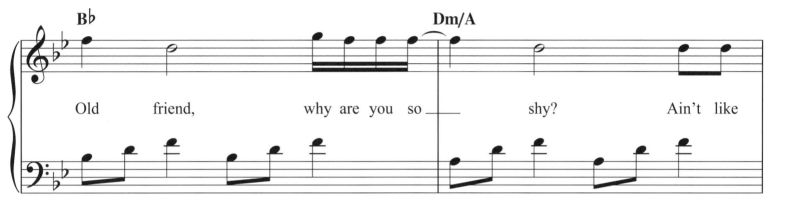

Old friend, why are you so ___ shy? Ain't like

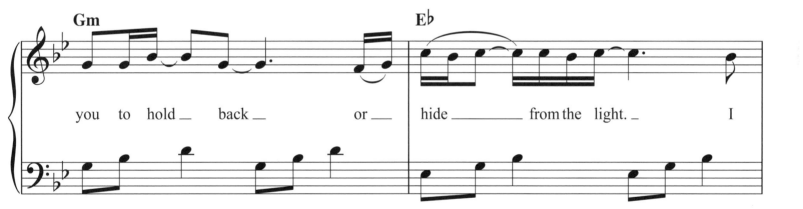

you to hold __ back __ or __ hide _____ from the light. _ I

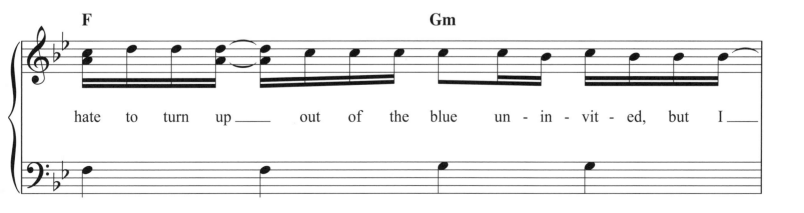

hate to turn up ___ out of the blue un-in-vit-ed, but I___

Eb

couldn't stay away, ___ I couldn't fight it. I had

F   Gm

hoped you'd see my face   and that you'd be re-mind-ed that, for

Eb

me, ___   it is-n't o - ver. ___

Bb   F   3   Gm   Eb

Nev-er mind,_ I'll find some-one like you.   I wish

noth - ing but ___ the best for you, too. Don't for -

get me, I beg. I re - mem - ber you said, "Some-times it

To Coda ⊕

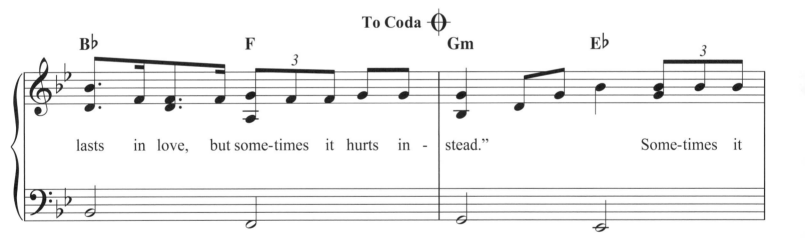

lasts in love, but some-times it hurts in - stead." Some-times it

lasts in love, but some - times it hurts in - stead. ___

You know how the time flies, on-ly

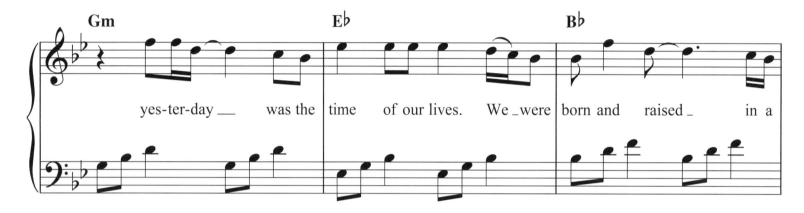

yes-ter-day ___ was the time of our lives. We _were born and raised _ in a

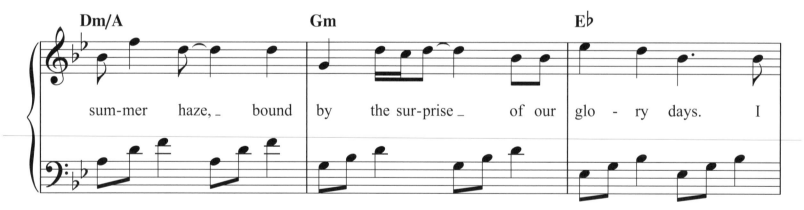

sum-mer haze,_ bound by the sur-prise _ of our glo - ry days. I

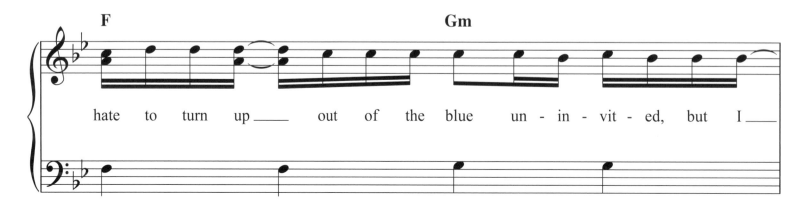

hate to turn up ___ out of the blue un-in-vit-ed, but I ___

_____ could-n't stay a - way, _____ I could-n't fight it. I had

hoped you'd see my face and that you'd be re - mind - ed that, for

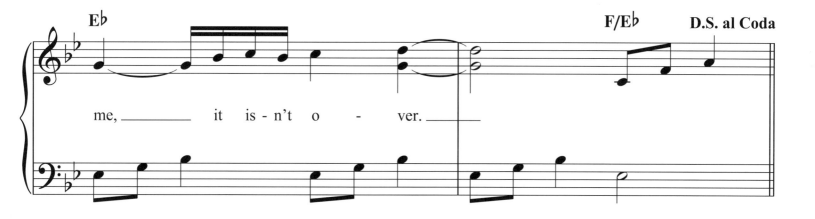

me, _____ it is - n't o - ver. _____

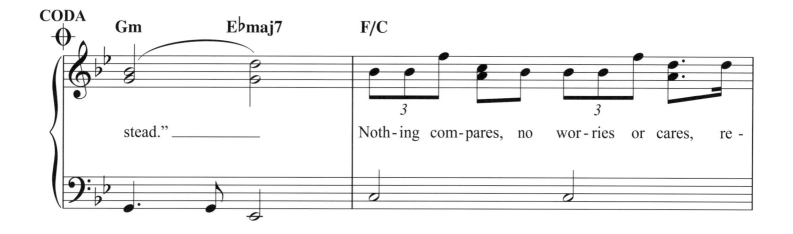

stead." _____ Noth-ing com-pares, no wor-ries or cares, re-

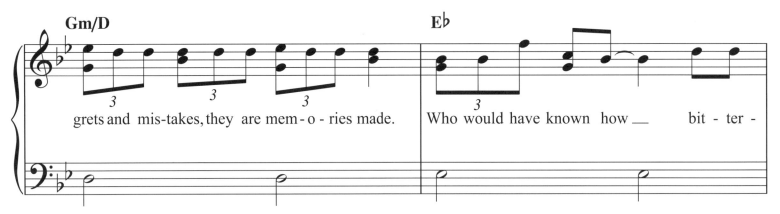

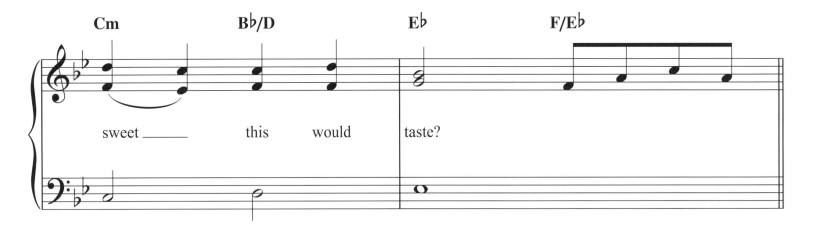

mem - ber   you said, "Some-times it   lasts   in love, but some-times it hurts in -

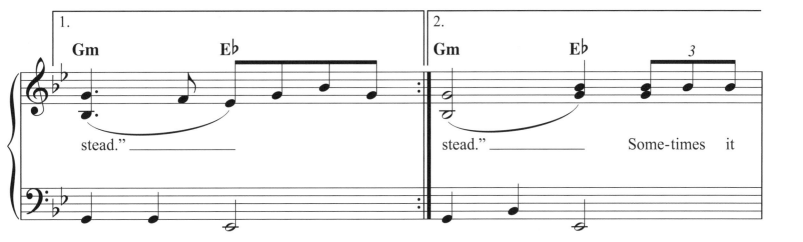

1.
stead." _____   2.   stead." _____   Some-times   it

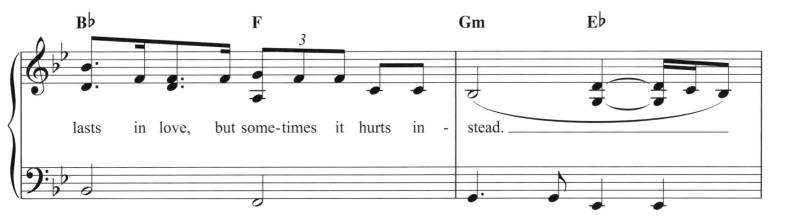

lasts   in love, but some-times it hurts in -   stead. _____

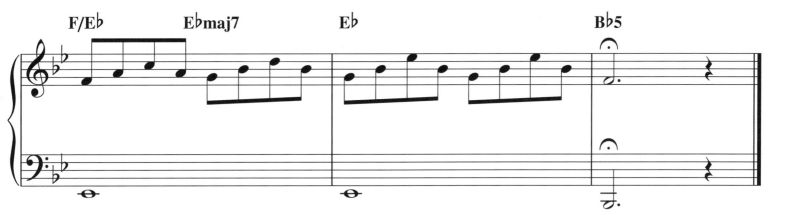

WHEN WE WERE YOUNG

Words and Music by ADELE ADKINS
and TOBIAS JESSO JR.

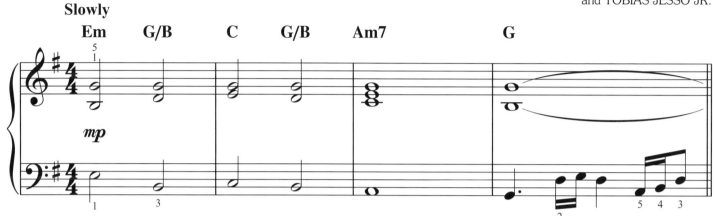

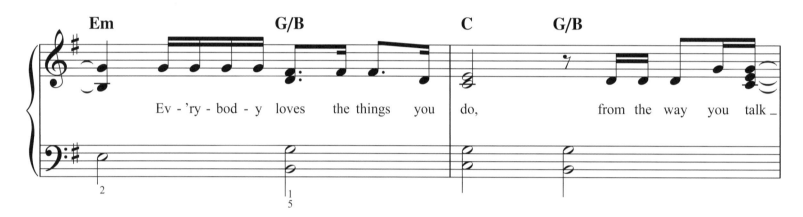

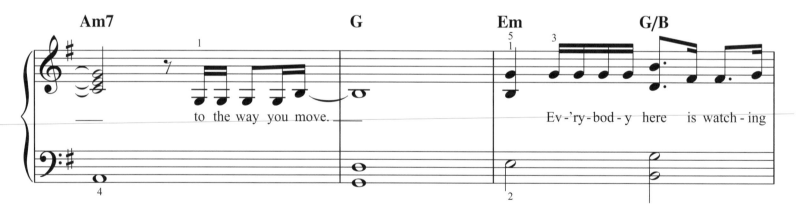

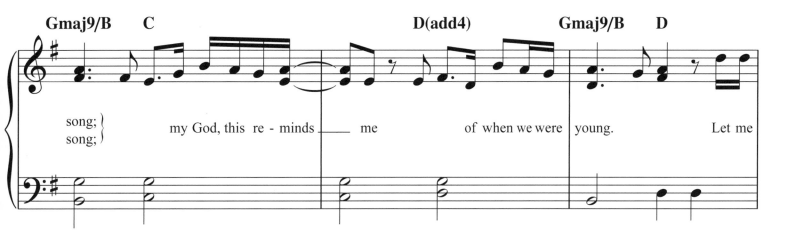

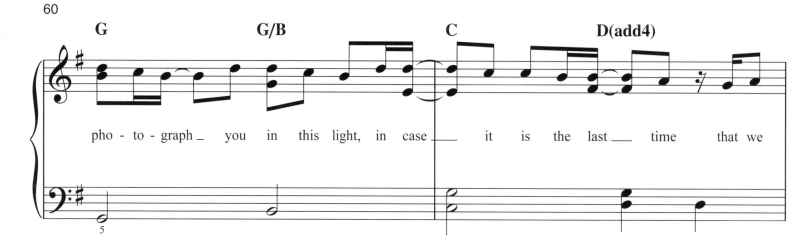

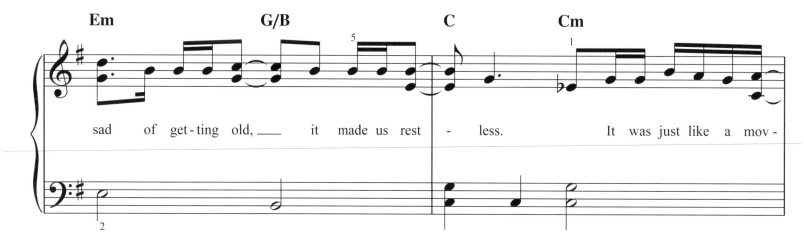

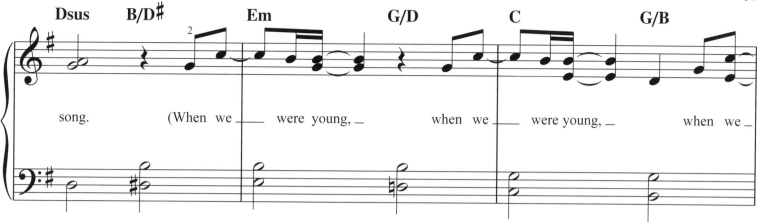

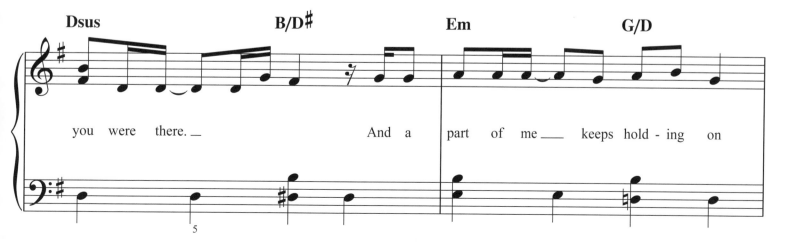

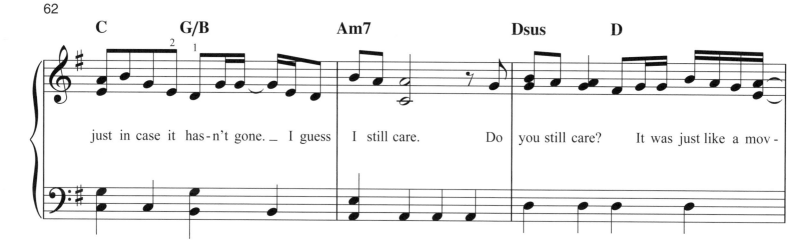

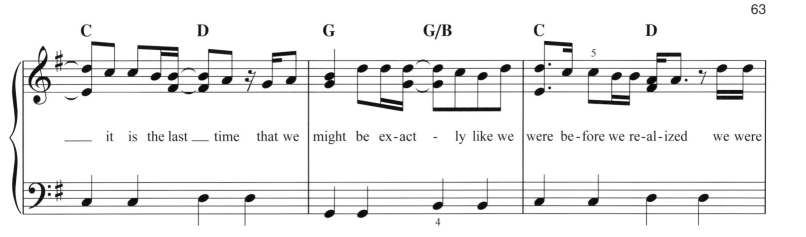

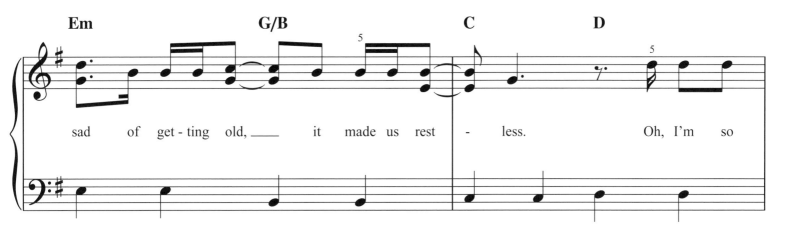

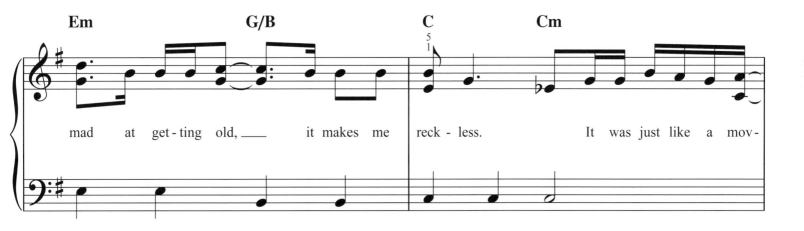